Coming to Terms with a Child

Coming to Terms
with a Child

Henry Beissel

Black Moss
Press
2011

Library and Archives Canada Cataloguing in Publication

Beissel, Henry, 1929-
Coming to terms with a child / Henry Beissel.

Poems.
ISBN 978-0-88753-489-8

I. Title.

PS8503.E39C65 2011   C811'.54   C2011-901312-6

Cover painting: Arlette Francière, The Terror of War, Acrylic, 16x12
Design: Kate Hargreaves

Black Moss
EST. 1969 **Press**

Published by Black Moss Press at 2450 Byng Road, Windsor, Ontario, N8W 3E8. Canada. Black Moss books are distributed in Canada and the U.S. by LitDistCo. All orders should be directed there.

Black Moss would like to acknowledge the generous financial support from both the Canada Council of the Arts and the Ontario Arts Council.

Canada Council   Conseil des Arts
for the Arts   du Canada

ONTARIO ARTS COUNCIL
CONSEIL DES ARTS DE L'ONTAR

Contents

to my grandson Bennett

1. Once upon a Time

Praise be to the years that unspooled
from the skein of uncertain destinies
hour by hour and month after month
the improbable stitch in time to mark
the spot where something popped to which
I am the sole survivor and the last witness.

Anniversaries are wayside inns to unfold
maps, confirm roads travelled and mark
routes yet to be explored: the eightieth calls
for a weather check as well, and time out
to tank new energies while puzzling over
aging monuments and promising geographies.

But maps don't tell the story of a life
even if memory could locate and describe
the thirty thousand dawns that roused me
from thirty thousand sleeps, even if it could

trace the thirty thousand lines light drew
along the edge of darkness, along the edge
of the river whose eddies and currents model
destiny – even if memory could connect
the dots dreams and nightmares left
across thirty thousand windows onto reality,
the resulting maps would still fail to chart
the unaccountable twists and turns, intricate
and intimate, a journey takes in a life
moving boldly, blindly from childhood
to old age knowingly ignorant.

Once upon a time and once only
then and there were here and now
but how to find them
behind so many veils and screens...

2. Country of Origin

Open a map of Germany and locate the city
of Cologne. Who could've known that a bend
in the river would become the colonial capital
of Rome's northern empire, acquire a cardinal's
hat and privileges, hatch from a clutch of churches
a cathedral to challenge heaven, then flourish
for a time as a port commanding one of Europe's
major shipping lanes before the iron horse
and the mechanical bird, before fossil-fed
monsters heated up the ancient games of greed
and power the few have always played with
the many, staking nations on a dare, banking
on turning strangers into scapegoats, whipping
generations into orgies of hatred and violence
till the whole continent caught fire and twice
in a single century even the honourable succumbed
to the poison of patriotism. Deluded by drill
and discipline they followed the false lead
of flags and marching bands herding the sheep

heroically to their slaughter and leaving Cologne
ingloriously in ruins – bombed into heaps of brick
scrap metal craters shells of homes broken doors
unhinged wall paper peeling across smashed tables
cracked kitchen sinks Dürer's *Hands* crushed
askew behind shattered glass collapsed floors
a toilet bowl open-mouthed as though petrified
at the height of a primal scream: ashes ashes
everywhere: the city 32 million cubic meters
of rubble where 262 air raids buried 20,000 dead –
and somewhere in among the debris the bruised
and battered dreams of a child turned into a nightmare.

Massacre of children and their mothers, of the sick
and the old, civilians mutilated to demoralize
the troops, dismembered, incinerated in numbers
ten times the days so far recorded in my life.
In the acrid incense of burning flesh a pathetic
God choked to death in his vomit, his blessings
cut to ribbons, his faith in rags of disbelief
as flames danced on the river whose dark waters
flowed silently under bridges linking firestorms.

To have survived this inferno is no more miraculous
than to have been born into it. The luck of a throw
of fate's dice assigns to each of us a country of origin,
the luck of countless draws between male and female
lined up all the way back into precambrian mists.
It's not always the fastest and most forceful sperm
that enters the egg; sometimes the dreamy-eyed
latecomer is admitted and the strongest shut out.
It seems that cells that have no mind have a mind

and meaning of their own. Every birth refutes
the law of probability by the caprice of conception
and survival. None of us should have come into being
in the first place, none could have been predicted.
Nor would I have chosen of all times and places
the time and place there and then. But you don't
negotiate chaos. In the casino of life too the odds are
stacked against you. To escape flying bullets or bombs
warrants no pride and no merit: you can't dodge them;
you wait and when you hear them, you're safe.
Their whistle lets you know they've missed you.
Only silent shrieks kill, shrieks for the lucky to hear.

I was not always so lucky in my dreams. There
they assaulted me for decades and woke me
in fear and panic for without a sound they found
their target. I died a thousand deaths and lived
to see another dawn when the sun slapped my face
back into affirmation. Slowly the years grounded
the Lancasters and Flying Fortresses. An uneasy
armistice came to prevail in the land of my dreams
after I moved to a world where war was hearsay.

Here vast solitudes are invaded only by the wind
and the dark skies flash only with dying comets
and the ghostly dances of northern lights. Night
now brings forgetting, offers coveted oblivion.
The bloodthirsty beasts of war swoop down on me
in broad daylight instead. They bear different names:
Bosnia, Chechnya, Iraq, Rwanda, Afghanistan
and Gaza, each of them recalling reenacting reviving
the surreal scenes I witnessed in those years of terror

and tyranny so bone-chillingly beyond belief and bearance
I can no longer be sure what fevered fear projects
on the walls of memory and what I experienced,
what panic stampedes into images and what I saw
turn ten thousand childhoods into one long nightmare.

3. It's always Today

I am writing this to you in my eighties – a long stretch
of yesterdays the inner ear must travel to catch
the fading echoes of a world as alien to you as the age
of the Pharaohs. I too stare bewildered at the maps
in my memory, find the routes travelled uncertain,
puzzling, the scenery hard to credit, and the monuments
by the wayside aging, paltry, tattered by the brutality
of experience. Yet the past is our only guide to the future:
dismiss it and you totter into a roadside ditch
like Brueghel's blind band of vagabonds. That's why
I'm trying to draw a map for you, a map of my early
travels, though I know it's always today and the reality
of what was and will be is different every day.

Forceps were needed to drag me screaming
into the cold dry light of April as though I knew
what was to come. In London, Jacob Epstein
was carving *Light* in stone when darkness
descended on the nations of Europe and became

the terror of my childhood. Nights filled with
demons that bared fire-spitting fangs and curled
vicious claws to threaten unnamable horrors
long before they became real monsters that spat
real flames and real bullets into real flesh.

Nights also taught me the grace of words to save me
from the black clutches of solitary darkness:
with parents gone out, alone in the flat at night
I was left to extemporize Cowboys and Indians,
plots and characters with enough thrill and suspense
to keep my untroubled brother awake as an ally
against the ghoulish denizens hovering in ambush
in every dark corner and behind every door, crawling
with slimy furtiveness across the ceiling. My fiction
was no match for the reality of my younger sibling's
somnolence and of the ghost-infested rooms I patrolled
fearfully turning on all the lights to prevent the fiends
from feasting on my flesh and on my childish anguish.

Sometimes night came in the middle of the day
as punishment for mischief never fully understood
and often patently unjust. As the older child I was
always guilty, innocence being undemonstrable. Down
in the black abyss of the windowless basement demons
wrestled me to the ground to lie among piles of coal
in the foul fumes of fermenting green beans, tears
mingling with coal dust to smear my face like a chimney
sweep, my cries baffled by fungi, roaches and mold
in the damp dirt lining raw brick walls – till something
wore out inside me, something withered to a whimper
as I tried to measure the burden of the penalty against

the weight of the offence. Perhaps my mother too
weighed the odds and found them wanting. I still hear
her descending that haunted staircase to rescue me
from her own mercurial anger mysteriously morphed to pity.

There were other nights – nights of beer and knives,
when the stress of the incompatible and the intolerable
broke into open warfare and my mother sought shelter
under my covers while my father knew not who he was
or what he was doing. Music turned into a cacophony
of incriminations as he discovered at the bottom
of a tankard of beer courage, jealousy – and shame.
Memory's lens is out of focus when turned upon
such scenes and there is never quite enough light –
just enough for a quick gleam on a bread knife,
an image etched black-and-white into a child's in-
comprehension between two adults' incoherent utterances.

Not far away the dark river twisted and turned
in its bed of rocks, muttering enigmatically.
Its waters could not clean the city's wounds
nor cool the fevers of the human heart and mind.

4. Dancer from the Unknown

If there is only today, why does yesterday so often squat
on my chest like a scowling gargoyle belabouring my breath?
Yesterday is no more chiseled in stone than tomorrow.
I am a counter on the abacus of time, both moved
and moving, trying to calculate losses against gains
that are the price of living in a season of blood.
Between firestorms and nightmares I search for a child's
innocence and enthusiasm that defy capricious fortune.

The time before the war comes in flashes obscured
by the bitter smoke of *Köln am Rhein* burning
in the foreground. No sight or sound issues
from my clandestine birth out of wedlock
in what was then a city with a sense of humour
that took only its carnival seriously – and sometimes
its religion. Scandal averted by being farmed out
to a wet-nurse, followed by a forced marriage
when the family discovered the infant I was
sanctified in church to restore respectability

and legitimize my existence as though life
were an edict of bureaucracy. I reject also
any responsibility for the crash on Wall Street
six months after I crashed into the world.
Black Thursday the baby was likely lying lily-white
in his cradle listening to his father, the pianist,
practicing Beethoven practicing Chopin Debussy
practicing practicing Brahms Ravel Mozart Schubert –
they were all the same to him, the same magic,
adagio or *allegro, pianissimo* or *forte, con brio*
they stirred his blood to song forever.

The years when the Papal See made peace
with evil and its bankers were lean years
for a musician still studying at the conservatory
but already with a wife whose education no one
wanted and all too soon a second son to rear. Bread
and butter were scarcer than sonatas and concerti.

When the veil of smoke, debris and fire trembles,
I see on the other side of devastation my father
late at night at the kitchen table, the lamp pulled
down just above his head, copying musical scores.
That and private piano lessons made for a wretched
living, and I see my mother weeping desperately
at the bailiff come to affix his seal on the piano
as security against unpaid bills, or sweet-talking
into credit for another week a haughty landlady
come imperiously to collect the rent. Exhausted
from endless days of washing and worrying, cooking
and caring for two boys, one more mutinous than
the other, my mother was deep in troubled sleep

during those midnight hours when the kitchen clock
was ticking away my father's life, wasting another
talent struggling to survive. Hunger was a frequent host
in our unheated flat while outside in the hooligan
streets drums and fanfares heralded a holocaust
for the nation of *Dichter und Denker*[1] as an Austrian
ex-corporal clawed his way to power – a psychopath
more representative of a psychopathic world than poets
and thinkers, or a pianist dreaming music, his fingers
on the pulse of an age no longer or not yet manifest.

Later, my mind struggling to focus, and months before
I could walk, they gave Leon Trotsky his walking papers
in Moscow. He walked the tightrope of his dissent
into exile where under a merciless sun years later
Stalin's ice-pick shattered his dreams of a fairer world
with one blow to the brain just as my own dreams
burst under the blows of a similar battle between power
and justice – the idiot tale of *Homo sapiens* called
history. Brute force vanquishes all that's noble in nature
and challenges delicate tendrils to cling to the wind.
From the beginning, my life, like my native city,
was stretched tight between the first word and the next
blow, between music and madness, art and politics,
for me to move like a dancer from the unknown
to the unknowable and learn to celebrate the day
as the river celebrates the sky all the way to the sea.

5. Never-ending Quest

Fortune's wheel turns and turns, driven by the winds
of change. We are the wings attached to its centre
by birth and being, suspended side to side and top
to bottom in the balance of fear and hope, flying
over the void beckoning from all directions between tears
and laughter to find grief and grandeur in the dark.

* Memoflash: a little brother who was still little then
and a brother / downhill on a sleigh / the Greenbelt white
with snow / a cold headwind screaming exuberance / I bite
the snow: sweet soft ice crunch – only children know
true winter bliss. * Memoflash: reading under the covers
at night *Schatzinsel*[2] and *Winnitou*[3] by flashlight / divine
fever of the imagination / fear of discovery and the strap
drowned in a tempestuous sea of adventures – closer
to paradise no human is permitted. * Memoflash: running
through fragrant pine woods / *Königsforst*[4] / we are kings
out hunting / pockets full of salt / amused adults animating
us / catch a rabbit by strewing salt on its tail / the weary rabbits

never sat still / we pick blueberries instead / mouths painted
mauve and large / circus clowns spreading fruity joy –
never was there a happier more loving *Oma.*[5] * Memoflash:
granny's coffee-mill / grinding half an ounce of dark
crackling beans / then cheating her at snakes and ladders /
she knew – her smile knew boys must always always win.
* Memoflash: my first opera, *Zar und Zimmermann*[6] /
I was ten / actors, makeup, costumes, singing / I was standing
up high amongst the gods / *Oh ich bin klug und weise
und mich betrügt man nicht!*[7] – I can still sing the arias
though I am neither clever nor wise and was even then
betrayed by those I trusted. *Die Worte sind von mir verfasst
in einer stillen Stunde.*[8] Lortzing's music survived the bombed-out
opera house, the bombed-out city, my bombed-out childhood.

A shaft of sunlight may yank you out of a dream,
out of bed and drop you in a meadow of euphoria
where you fly a kite larger than yourself. A photo
shows you holding a kite with a swastika pasted on it.
In a world of want and pain, is every moment of joy
tainted with shame? Must one be ignorant to be
happy? What was I looking for the night I climbed
out of the window to wander the streets in pyjamas?
Escaping demons in the home or in the prison
of my skin? Searching for my parents in the pub
around the corner? The dark was raw and threatening.
A kind-hearted, helmeted policeman took me home
again, helped me climb back through the ground-floor
window where my little brother was still asleep.

There were the rare evenings I begged *Vati und Mutti*[9]
to play Sinding's *Frühlingsrauschen,*[10] begged

and badgered till they fetched the extra chair
from the kitchen: four hands on the piano conjured
a rustling breeze of spring, flooded the flat
and wafted me to sweet dreams in a landscape
momentarily bathed in sunlight because I understood
what was broken between father and mother was mended
by the magic of the music. In that brief *arpeggio* run
of time they found harmony and happiness. It was as if
springwaters had flooded a river's banks and meadows
burst into blossom and birdsong. I did not know that
at the same time in Cologne and in other cities and towns
across the country brownshirt barbarians were tearing
other families apart, their hobnailed boots trampling
into dust everything true and tender that rough hands
and raw hearts had nurtured to life over centuries.
Years passed before the world's cruel truths came
home to haunt me into outrage, shame and exile.

6. How Thorny the Path

Easter 1935. His first school day.
In Korea, a teenager, Sun Myung Moon,
praying on a mountain top, chose to be
God's son, his true Messiah, come late
to establish God's kingdom on earth.
In Cologne, along the banks of the Rhine,
a toddler, starry-eyed, *Schultüte*[11] half full
of candy and cookies, stood innocently
at the foot of the mountain of knowledge
to set out on the never ending climb
to the peak. Neither the toddler nor
the teenager knew the pilgrimage
of learning passes through the only kingdom
on earth that will last forever, for life itself
is learning to share and exchange information.

Little did the little boy know how thorny the path
was to the triple Rs. A hunchback. *Stand to
attention!* The morning ritual. *Heil Hitler!* If only

instead of hailing him someone had healed him
before he barred and bolted his humanity away
with his hatred in the metal-plated vault of his skull
and chose to be the nation's redeemer – another
one of God's power-drunk appointees. *Sit down!*
The hunchback was the teacher. He taught
with the rod. And with cold fury. Ten strokes
across the palm of the hand for not adding up right
or not spelling right or not writing neat. It hurt
to hold the *Griffel*[12] after that. *Sit still! Get out
your slates!* First rule: obey! *Copy the blackboard!*
The squeak of slate scratching slate gave him
goose-pimples. *No talking! You're here
to learn.* Discipline – *Disziplin über alles*!
Rules are rules he discovered when the ruler
came down hard. *Drop you pants! Bend over!
I'll make men of you yet.* I can still hear the hiss
of the rod, feel the welts that made sitting
in the narrow wooden bench torture.
Prussian overture to the glories of learning.

But there is that in us that survives
the fallacies and delusions of our elders –
some force that brought the single cell
from the primal slime across aeons
of catastrophes by asteroid, volcanoes
and polar ice to form colonies by the trillions
that learnt to fly and sing and wonder.

That's what drove the little boy – awe
and wonder at being alive there and then
surrounded by miracles and mysteries

of such ravishing beauty and raw brutality
he just had to learn to fly and sing
to come to terms with himself and the world.
With such determination learning came easy
and he ran the gauntlet of hunchbacks
blinded by tears he groped in the darkness
of his spirit and discovered joy beyond the pain
as he climbed the mountain to be who he was.

7. Not a Fairytale

Children are most at home in play, the rules
of the game their measure of time and space.
Their universe is rounded by the ball they throw,
kick or catch, by the arc of a swing or the circle
they draw in the sand. Here and now are home.
Caught in a web of their own making, connected
unwittingly to all things. Engagement casts a spell
that banishes before and after. The day reality
rudely breaks the circle, innocence is shattered
and the thread is cut by which the world hung
seemingly harmless and joyful in a child's grasp.

Once upon a time there was a little boy who discovered paradise.
He came upon it in a spring garden behind a village inn
far outside the city limits: a swing hidden in a tiny sandpit
as in a bower of blooming shrubs and lush flower beds.
A fancy swing! With padded seat, guard rail and safety chain!
Suspended between heaven and earth from a steel frame
by thick ropes that in his hands became a ladder to pull

himself up to the clouds. All alone he soared jubilantly
under fragrant linden trees, by bright blue morning glory
into stippled canopies, swinging up and down for hours,
back and forth like some ancient pendulum measuring eternity...
till his spirit was free – free from the weight of his body
from the weight of his thoughts he swung higher and higher
gloriously into the sky propelled by the thrill of the dare
he almost completed a circle screaming in fearful bliss
almost upside down in the blue air it was flight it was freedom
it was euphoria that prompted him to jump from the height
of his ecstasy – an instant of rapture, a sharp pain in his groin,
and he lay bleeding in the sand, his pants and his penis torn:
the hook of the safety chain had brought his manhood up short.

He came to on a white sheet, his aunt the nurse holding
his hand, telling him softly everything's alright, it's only
a bit of skin, the doctor has fixed it between pain and oblivion
drifting without understanding only when the ether let go
of his consciousness he felt his *Pipimännchen*[13] heavily bandaged,
raw, sore, a dark fear crept up his spine and into his skull,
it smelled of vomit, his childish flesh goose-pimpled –
something was wrong with the world, some evil was lurking
in the splotches of sunshine pushing through the slats of the blinds
in the doctor's office, some evil giant bending over him, hurting him,
putting him, too early, too guileless, on his guard forever.

Years later he had all but forgotten. Nature had healed
his wounds. Obedient to the dictates of his pride, memory
let him off the hook, replacing a foolish jump with an unfortunate
fall. But time's healing powers are circumscribed by malice.
Du hast ja keine Vorhaut![14] roared the *Fähnleinführer*[15]
in command at the Hitler Youth camp, pointing at his genitals.

Du bist ein Judenlümmel![16] His bark echoed across the steaming
crowded shower room: *Judenlümmel Judenlümmel! Judenlümmel!*
The other boys joined in the outrage, gloating at the opportunity
to excoriate the nerd amongst them: revenge for his troublesome
presence repudiating their smug normalcy – reading books!
which they read as a rebuke to their banality, as though he were
trying to be something better, someone special... His hands tried
to cover where everyone was staring. *It's no use trying
to hide it!* shrilled the brown shit uniform. *We've all seen it!
You're circumcised! Only Jews are circumcised!* He couldn't
understand, stammered, he had never known a real Jew
nor heard of circumcision ever, but he was terrified, he knew
from the voice the raucous voice on the radio it was not good
to be a Jew and he knew mob hysteria from party rallies
when all hell broke loose with forests of flags and brass bands.
In vain he tried to explain what he did not understand. Jeering,
pushing and cuffing, they took him away, put him under
Stubenarrest[17] – till his parents produced a valid *Ahnenpass*[18]
to prove stamped and sealed two hundred years of Aryan ancestry.

How he wished he had been born
in a different age and a different place –
an age and a place of fairytales! He would've
sailed down the Rhine in a schooner
down to the sea and beyond to fairyland
where he might have been an Oriental prince,
rich, handsome, just, who travelled the world
in disguise, bighearted and openhanded
to his subjects but merciless with evildoers.
Little did the dreamer know his ancestors
on their slow move from darkest Africa
spent millennia in the hills of Galilee

before migrating north. Little did he know
that he had to be who and where and when he was –
a slave chained to the galley of his fate –
and to accept it or he would not be at all.

8. Pieces of the Puzzle

Stare, stare in the mirror and watch
the pretender make a thousand faces
as he picks and chooses from a jar
brimful with the ills and evils of his age
trying to fit pieces together into a whole,
a jigsaw puzzle of his identity and his past.
He turns each fragment everywhich way
until it clicks into place; some fit every
where, others nowhere, leaving lacunae
large enough to hide a thousand lives.

Look closely and you can see already
he regrets having opened the lid, but
such is his punishment for prying
into the secrets of the gods' fire: he must
dig deep down to the bottom of the jar
to find, like Pandora, a well concealed
crusty layer of hope that needs scraping
loose and soaking in tears. He refuses pity

and stares, stares defiant in the mirror.
If this is the face that haunts his nights
he'll stick his tongue out and curse all that
is senseless and irreconcilable as he praises it:
Go ahead, Zeus, show off your childish thunder
and lightning games! You know no more who
you are or what you got involved in than I do.
For all that, I prefer the candle to the flash:
flickering through the foxholes of memory
it plays with light and shade like a prelude
by Debussy my father played against the war.

Darkness. The train rattles and shakes the night. People weary hungry sitting standing dozing in crammed carriages. Sour smell of sweat and fear. Lights out. Enemy planes overhead. I stand squished between strangers: an old man with cane, dazed soldiers on leave, women in search of food, safety, escape, refugees from city air raids, children, like myself... A hand strokes my hair, briefly caresses my cheek, moves quickly down to fuss with my fly... I look up, catch a leer in a soldier's eye, turn away confused... my hand is gripped pulled to touch clammy flesh shaft I feel sick tear myself away... – A thunderous detonation! The train stops violently. Boxes tumble from racks. Metal screams at metal. Bodies surge forward. We tumble on top of each other. Yelling. Crying. Windows break. Doors open. The cold night air is sobering. People plunge down the embankment. Anti-aircraft guns bark ferociously. Dark figures running panic-stricken for a nearby patch of forest. Night fighter bombers overhead. There's no escape. The indifferent stars watch with cold eyes. I'm in a hot sweat... – Daylight. Where am I? Lying in a patch of wild grass in a forest clearing. A young officer hands me a photo. Nude woman. Exposed. Pink nipples. Stiff. Pink cleft. Stiff. Exposed. He. The sun dances fondles kisses. The glistening tip of my... No, no, I'm stealing along a dark creaking corridor. Sweating. Mustn't wake the old man and his hag. A grandfather clock strikes midnight. I'm trembling. The pretty maid is waiting. In a translucent slip. Slippery. Waiting for me in bed. Soft. Softly. To show me. Between the sheets. Soft touch the first the sight the first time her breasts naked raise a storm in my blood in her arms she shares with me the secrets of the god's fire in the loin and yes yes the candle has been burning ever since, still burns in the cave of my desires. – *Go get a bowl of whipping cream from the baker, Heinz. I've baked a pound-cake; it's Sunday.* Oh, mother! You passed the torch on to me, but you never told me the secret. That you should've died such a painful death! Though I chose not to be there I shared your pain through long months, even woke in an Irish night screaming at dying! Connemara put a bullet in my brain. I don't know how but we stayed connected across thousands of miles of thought and experience separating us. Still the rustle of spring stirs my blood, yes I still burn candles in my heart for you and yes at dawn in my solitude... I sometimes hear the schmaltzy operetta arias you wept over. *Stopfkuchen mit Schlagsahne!*[19] I learnt too late the banal can be a language of love.

Close the lid on your jar, Pandora,
and padlock it. The past lies shredded
in your judgment. Remembrance
is as capricious as fortune
and as contrary as Schrödinger's cat.
You pull from the jumble of synaptic
flashes strands to pattern a world
that was an illusion even when
it existed. They told him love
conquered all, but he learnt better.
They taught him only to make war

and give death its bloody dominion
to make him a man, and he became
a man in fits and starts though he was
still a lifetime away from understanding
that manhood is not a stiffening in the groin
but an embrace of frailty and a stiffening
of resolve in the face of the world's charge.

When the shelter's meter-thick walls
swayed in a hail of bombs, the lights
went out and women sobbed and prayed
he ran out into the noisy street
and looked up at the sky glittering
with bright flares and bursting shells.

There was no one to hear him scream
above the deafening explosions
as he watched the rigid fingers
of searchlights probing thick clouds
like the pale hand of a dying god
drawing attention to his plight,
beckoning a drone of birds of death
and destruction to their doom
and waving goodbye to the earth.

Was this the time he came to know
life has no meaning beyond death?
And that the talking animal
is an impostor with forked tongue
to deceive himself and the world?
At the edge of the abyss he learnt
there are no edges, only transitions,

the river runs on relentlessly
and returns the rains to the sky.
He discovered the abyss inside himself.

Let not the piano mislead you:
its black-and-white keys may move you
to a world in measured order,
but light and shade are not counterpoints;
they're singer and accompanist.
Music has no morals: it can open or shut
the gates separating harmony from mayhem.

9. Hither and Thither

When war broke out, he was on a farm
in a village up north near the Free City of Bremen
that, unbeknownst to him, was no longer free
because the town musicians[20] turned out to be
real witches, ogres, giants and dragons and
they all wore excrement-brown uniforms.
He loved the much more colorful musical tale
of the donkey, the cat, the dog and the rooster.
Every day he rode into the same world
of adventure on horseback on the farm every day
riding bareback he flew in the wind whistling freedom
to the rhythm of hooves drumming the meadow.
He knew nothing of war. They said it'd be over
in a couple of weeks. It sounded like another
kind of game. That's all he could think of –
escape from the city from home from school
to the exhilaration of summer in the country.[21]
It took years of aerial bombardment for the game
to become too serious and frightening to be fun.

The year *Stukas*[22] bombed Warsaw he was awarded
a high school scholarship. Little did the boy know
that both changed his world forever and that he would
shake with terror to the same hail of bombs that shook
little Jaroslaw in the city which was in the news when
he was horseback riding blissful across the fields
of Lilienthal.[23] After that the path of higher learning
turned into an odyssey on the tempestuous seas of WWII.
Cast hither and thither among different schools
between bombed out buildings at home, evacuation
to cities now Polish, and refugee escapes, he became
a wandering student, never long enough anywhere
to make friends, and always pulled and pushed
in a different direction from year to year, each school
with a different mission: Latin to train his thoughts to leap
to the laws of logic; English to prepare him for a future
neither his teacher nor himself could have imagined;
the sciences to fuel his appetite for knowing how and why
that rendered him incapable of ever understanding boredom;
and literature to push open windows on all sides in the tower
of his mind and reveal a landscape crowded with confused
people in search of something they lost when they found it.

* Memoflash: the day I played hooky in grade 3 to make the rounds
with the iceman / lugging chunks of ice up three or four flights
of stairs for a nickel or a dime / that day the class went to the zoo
and they had sent for me / my distraught mother worried to death
all morning waiting / hysterical / *Wo warst Du?*[24] / pretended
innocence / tried to lie my way out of it / she slapped my face
hard. – Lies have short lives.* Memoflash: the short pudgy math
teacher / thick-lipped with a lisp / always repeated his last phrase
softly / taught philosophy too / my favorite subject / irked him

by showing no interest in math (because there was always only one easy correct answer, unlike in real life) / admonished me: *Mathematik ist auch Philosophie* (then faintly like an echo) *ist auch Philosophie.* – Too late I discovered how true this was. * Memoflash: the bearded one-eyed biology teacher / explaining the function of a monkey's tail / we giggled in our teens: for a tail is a *Schwanz* is a penis / furious he picked the next best for punishment: me / held my face with one hand and hit it with the other / to compensate for his glass eye / struck my cheek with full force / I hated him with all my heart and wished him dead / later that afternoon he fell from a plum tree in his garden and died / from internal injuries / my curse? – If hatred has such power, does the same apply to love?

Adults were beyond his understanding. They worshipped
a god of love who expressly forbade killing: Thou Shalt Not
slaughter men, women and children wholesale.
Yet they slowly reduced Cologne, city of churches,
to an arena of rubble and ruins. Every night was carved
into slices of fear by sirens, anti-aircraft cannon
and bombs, carpets of bombs dropped to kill
and destroy all. In the day Lancasters took over
the job from Flying Fortresses. Whole neighbourhoods
wiped out in a storm of fire. Classmates buried
under the rubble. School did not prepare him for hell.
Its subjects seemed irrelevant to the world's reality.
The teenager struggling to discover himself lost
interest in school learning. Permanently tired
and undernourished, he might have shipwrecked
had not two drunken sailors beaten him within an inch
of his life. His body might have washed up in the harbour
but for the inscrutable caprice of outrageous fortune.

The time would come when he felt guilty
for having survived the nightmare
of his childhood when bombs and bullets
buried so many who deserved better.

10. Cave Paintings

War smokes out the last vestiges of innocence,
even in a child. Its fires blister the thin skin
of their virtues, and burns images to make
the flesh creep into their sleep. Mine are
painted in human blood on the walls of a cave
still reverberating with the hysterical exhortations
of a clubfoot demagogue: *Wir wollen den totalen*
Krieg![25] and the roar of a frenzied deluded crowd:
Sieg Heil! Sieg Heil![26] as they blustered to defeat
and disgrace. *Räder müssen rollen für den Sieg!*[27]
But the nation ended up under the wheels
of trains that took its humanity to crematoriums.
Final solutions are not the fruit of violence and cruelty;
they grow only in the gardens of kindness and compassion.

All wars have their promoters on every side –
the dregs of humanity rising to call the shots,
the killer instinct grimacing on imagination's throne.
Their eyes leering sideways at the not so petty

cash, they poison the gullible with their rhetoric
of courage and honour concealing their predatory
prejudice. How else could a sane man or woman
be led to volunteer as paid killers and cannon
fodder for addicts of privilege and power? How about
their God who said *Thou shalt not kill*? He carved it
in stone, then put His signature on every soldier's
buckle: *Gott mit uns*.[28] *In God we trust*: impartially
he supports the carnage on every side, his pious servants
with their mouths full of *Te Deums* blessing the bombs
and passing the munition, then dipping their hands
in holy water to wash off the blood
in the name of the Father, the Son and the Holy
logic that sanctifies slaughter they celebrate a mass
for the dead pontificating about everlasting peace
when our cities lie in ruins and the killing fields
and forests are soaked with the blood of millions.
Oh, don't talk to me of war and its heroics!
War is always evil, especially when it looks good
and godly: its heroes lack the courage to be human.

Aerial combat over the Western front.
We 15-year-olds pause,
lean on our shovels and watch,
thankful for the excuse to stop
digging trenches
for strategic defence.
The roar and wail of engines
excite ancient instincts.
Like giant insects
two fighter planes twist
and turn

in death-defying circles
about each other
trying
to deliver a fatal sting.
Machinegun fire
rips the sky.
A jungle leaps to life
inside us.
It seems a fair fight.
We cheer: victory is in the air.
Messerschmidt & Spitfire
fly at each other
like crazed cocks
circle loop roll pull-up plunge
engines roaring
guns blazing
– suddenly
a wing disintegrates
in a puff of fire!
The plane nosedives
trails black smoke
hits the ground
explodes ... a moment
of uneasy silence ...
then a roar of hurrahs
from the horde of teenage conscripts
follows the departing victor.
We rush to the crash site:
a crater exhales noxious fumes
after spewing bits and pieces
of torn metal – the plane
shredded like an incriminating document

scattered in the field. There –
a lump of raw flesh
stuck to a broken piece of fuselage!
The pilot's final effort.
Over here – a hand
fingers curled
as though playing the piano
a waterproof watch still ticking
on the wrist
attached to half a forearm
severed where the elbow
should be
blood
oozing
... –
My stomach heaves,
I turn away and catch sight
of the twisted remnants
of the plane's markings:
an iron cross!
We cheered our own defeat:
the Spitfire had triumphed.
Inside me a jungle
filled with the howls
of vanquished ancestors
and vomited heroics.

Pastiche of a virtual reality where the body parts
of dismembered warriors ooze blood back to earth –
red river winding its way through the wild landscapes
of history carrying images that break down the doors
of perception or else darkness overtakes you and breaks
the cycle the seasons wheel about the void you occupy.

By that smoldering crater
by that oozing blood
I determined to live.

Perhaps the doctor who tore the nail from my big toe
saved my life. Conscription postponed for recovery.
Or was it the father of a school friend who lied for us
and sent us into hiding under cover of darkness?
When the *Stellungsbefehl*[29] caught up with me, I refused
to join the final total frenzy of defeat: men too old
to love a woman, boys who knew not yet how to.
With *Panzerfaust,*[30] rifles, munition belts and backpacks
full of apathy and capitulation they trudged away
from the advancing enemy. Day and night the sky
rained hellfire on the wretched remnants of a routed
army. *Sic transit gloria patriae.*[31] Smart goose-step
turned to tired slouch. Except for the roving raving
execution commandos hanging or shooting suspected
deserters with heel-clicking discipline and peppy glee.
I saw teenagers swinging in the wind from a noose
and knew Germany had come to the end of its rope.

I refused to die for a fatherland that deprived me
of a father when I most needed him: missing
in action; my mother wounded, narrowly escaping
death in an air raid, seeking protection from a Nazi
goat; my brother shot in the leg by a Mustang...
There is no home to defend where there is no family.
They sent me away from Köln where I was born –
dat is jät wo isch stolz drop bin,[32] sent me east
of the river winding through the skeleton of my city
like a silver ribbon sparkling in the sun and tying me

to streets, squares, schools, churches and soccer fields
that are now memories in the fading light of age.
There, in a village in the hills far east of my childhood,
I hid in a cellar, among familiar heaps of coal where
the monsters of my nightmares came home to roost
frightening me with grimaces of fear and foreboding –
till Roosevelt died on my 16th birthday and American
tanks roared down Marienheide's only thoroughfare
to smash and grind my world to dust. Freedom
I did not know or understand seized me by the throat
and choked the old life out of me, leaving me dazed
and destitute in a no-man's land of the heart and mind,
determined to absent myself forever without leave.

Yesterday is always another life
but when it's mired in oppression
the past becomes a succubus
to drive you to extinction – unless
another throw of fate's inscrutable dice
comes up with a winning number.

11. O Music!

And yes he had marched with them, marched *Vorwärts!*
Vorwärts![33] The bright blare of trumpets had called him,
ignited a passion in him for a better future no danger
was grave enough to stop him flags flying he was marching
they were all marching united and uniformed marching
into the future they believed *durch Nacht und durch Not*
marching *mit der Fahne der Jugend für Freiheit und Brot.*[34]

Yes he was carrying the flag of his youth through darkness
and sorrow into a new age of freedom and bread. He'd known
hunger and yes he was marching for a world where no one
went hungry and everyone was free yes he sang with all
the passion of his ignorant youth he and the other pre-teens
seduced by the music the primal rhythms the strident chorus
singing marching blasting words into the world they failed
to understand –
                    O music, elixir of the sublime! If
in some unimaginable n^{th} dimension there are gods of sound
they must be soaring through the architectonic spaces of a Bach

cantata or fugue, dancing to the melodic ecstasies of a Mozart
sonata, through the chambered transcendencies of Beethoven
deaf and dying, they must be singing with myriad voices
the muscular magnificence of Händel, the dulcet harmonies
of Schubert's yearning Lieder or *de profundis* the restless joyous
melancholy of Mahler –

                              But what do they make of the brutal beat
of tribal barbarism delivered at decibels that devastate the cochlea
and batter heart and mind to silence all that is good, gentle and true?
Is that why the gods have fallen silent? Singing gives even mortals
voices of angels, but not wrenched by the *GrößteFeldherrallerZeiten*[35]
to jangle and screech, amplified by the whining megalomania
of a false prophet deformed body and soul with a devil's mark.
If music be the wine that imbues free spirits with a thirst
for comprehension and compassion, one drop of poison
is enough to blind us and stop the feeling heart in its track.

Thus he marched and was marched
to drums, fanfares and flags
proclaiming the dawn
of *Freiheit und Brot*[36]
as tyranny took root
and he would have gone on
marching till his world
crumbled to ruin around him
but for one card in the hand
chance had dealt him at birth:
obstinacy, a refusal to obey,
a stubborn insistence to decide
for himself for better or for worse
what to do or not to do and live
or die with the consequences.

If he had understood that then,
he would not have lived to tell the tale.

There was his father's music
which transported him to the heart
of solitude and let him share it
with all who have ears to hear.
And there were the drums and fifes
of marching-bands that led the way
straight to perennial killing fields.

Music too, like time, is a river
that regenerates what it drowns.

12. *Danse macabre*

The day a world collapses is the day
another world is conceived.
It should've been All Fools' Day,
but chance never gets things quite right,
not even in retrospect. There should've been
a bang to end it all, followed by a whimper
to start it all over again. Instead,
the past petered out, surrendered
with the retreat of a rag-tag army
and the future came roaring in
on the wings of fighter-bombers
and in the chains of Sherman tanks.
How to negotiate the desperate
emptiness between them?

It was touch and go and the boy
deserter might have starved
to death in a POW camp,
but he learnt to translate

one world into another. Never
had he eaten so much and such
strange meals: hamburgers – had not
Hamburg perished in a firestorm?! –
with mashed potatoes soaked in gravy,
corn, crackers, peanut butter – all piled
in a single mess tin with pudding,
cookies and chunks of fruit in syrup
from the field kitchen for G.I.s.
A kraut teen lined up with them
while in the broken stone wilderness
of leveled cities pale emaciated
faces haunted the ruins like ghosts
in search of loved ones (and love),
frantic for food, water, coal –
those who chanced to survive
grasping for any line on life.

Cigarettes and whiskey, coffee
and chocolate were the currency
of the new world. His army
rations were the safe conduct
to survival for his mother
and his brother as he interpreted
and negotiated between occupiers
and occupied black market deals:
– a bottle of *Black and White* plus
a pound of coffee for a fur coat,
– a gold watch or a diamond ring
for a carton of *Players* and a box
of *Cadbury* bars – and a packet
of *Lucky Strike* would buy

many a lucky strike with many
a blond *Fräulein* for the whole night.

It was a *danse macabre* that brought
conqueror and conquered together
in an unacknowledged admission
of their common folly. And he was cock
of the dunghill, straddling both
sides of the equation, indulging
an appetite for life that became more
ferocious as he lost it to the horrors
of the thousand-year childhood
that stole his soul. He surrendered
to the adolescent roller-coaster ride
up women and down whiskey
till he reached the bottom
of the pit of despair that smelled
of natural gas and gun powder –
two epiphanies in the self's hell
where anguish wrestled lust
(How could the bullet have missed?
Who opened the window before
he passed out and on?) until the morning
after an orgiastic night, beaten
unconscious and robbed, spattered
with blood and vomit he came to
in the rubble of a torched city
not knowing where or who he was.

A look in the mirror revealed
a crack in the skull: two faces
at a crossroads: a parting of ways,

one up, one down, and he knew
the way up was not the same
as the way down, he understood
for the first time in his life
he had a choice – and he chose.

It had been a year of defeat, loss,
battery and a guilt too monstrous
for him to understand or bear.
For the first time he came to know
the meaning of Auschwitz,
Belsen, Buchenwald, Dachau,
Theresienstadt: he saw the piles
of naked corpses bulldozed into burial pits,
saw on film the skeleton survivors
of a massacre too gruesome
to contemplate – but contemplate it
he must, and struggle to come to terms
with barbarism. Millions of innocent
Jews disenfranchised persecuted tortured!
A people who, like no other, enriched
the nation and, indeed, the world
with intellectual and artistic triumphs
herded into cattle cars: men, women
and children taken to medical
experiments, firing squads, gas ovens
– EXTERMINATED!

Millions? Erased from the city, from their families,
from the earth? Without anyone noticing?
What about the neighbours? He stumbled over the facts.
How could he not have noticed? Afterwards

he saw the small squares – bronze plaques
like cobblestones, they call them *Stolpersteine,*[37]
hammered into the sidewalk outside houses
from where the Gestapo hauled their victims
to their death – daily reminders of our shame.
I found 15 memorial plates in front of a single
house facing the square where he used to play
with his friends: soccer, catch-me-if-you-can...
Hier wohnte
ARON FREUND
Jg. 1929
deportiert 1941
ermordet[38]
Born the same year I was, he did not survive
his twelfth year. Did he ever play with us?
I don't remember any Aron. But now I know
he was one of millions – Jews murdered by race
regardless of age or gender along with hundreds
of thousands of gypsies, communists, homosexuals,
trade unionists, Jehovah's Witnesses, freemasons,
dissenters and opponents, the handicapped –
all declared *Untermenschen,*[39] rounded up,
delivered forcibly to concentration camps
where the nation's uniformed scum
disposed of them like so much refuse.
A scene more savage than Dante's *Inferno*
enacted in the name of *Übermenschen!*[40]

Thus I learnt to beware of those
who claim supremacy of any kind:
they hide daggers in their rhetoric.

13. Descent

Something broke inside this 16-year-old
and he knew his heart could never forgive
himself for not doing what he could
not have done. It would never stop
weeping till it stopped beating.
He wanted to run and keep running
from the ruins of his illusions:
how could such depraved savagery
be perpetrated, ignored, condoned
by a nation of poets and thinkers?
How can anyone
release
c y a n i d e ! ! !
into a chamber packed
with naked women and children
and then listen to Beethoven's *Ode to Joy*
proclaiming *alle Menschen werden Brüder*[41]
and offering *diesen Kuss der ganzen Welt?*[42]

He was betrayed by those he trusted –
his parents, his priests, his teachers,
in whose care he had placed his tender
spirit. He was revolted by them as much
as by himself. Why had he not seen
what he had sensed? Had he looked
the other way? Despite his hostility?
Did he really see kindness in the face
of depravity and fail to notice the dagger
in those dark stabbing eyes? Would he,
one or two years older, have listened
to his inner voice? Was not survival
proof of cowardice beyond a reasonable
doubt in the court of his conscience?

There were no answers or he could not
find them because he did not know
the right questions. He searched everywhere
but found no solace in the familiar
world: two atomic bombs massacred
the innocent in Hiroshima and Nagasaki,
killed them instantly, or painfully slowly
and as gratuitously as the firestorms
of Dresden, Hamburg and Köln fried
tens of thousands of civilians – images
from the hell scenes of Hieronymus Bosch.
That too was the work of *Homo sapiens*.

He now descended into the basement
of his spirit where his soul crawled
into the darkest corner of his being.
There had to be a flaw in the neocortex,

some disconnect that allowed the rhetoric
of lunatics to turn humans into savages
more beastly than any beast. The brain
a terminal cancer perhaps? He decided
to flee from the site of his childhood
to the other side of an ocean
of a continent the other side
of his nightmares
though he knew there was no escape.
His eyes would retain and see
these images even in his grave.

Like a wounded animal he withdrew
into solitude wishing for the wisdom
of a colony of ants or the tender care
in a pride of lions. Twice he lay down
to let his demons carry him off. But
chance, cowardice and an absurd will
determined otherwise. At age 18, beaten
back to this absurd world within an inch
of everlasting peace, he began to engineer
his escape from the monsters of the past.
He stood on the bridge over the river
of his birth and cast his lot blindly
on the muddy waters of the future
carrying him across an ocean
to the shores of another, a new world.

14. Out of Darkness

There he stands, arms akimbo,
and lords it over my memory
claiming to be me. But he died
that drunken night in the ruins
of Hamburg, beaten unconscious
and robbed, his skull cracked
he died singing *Deutschland,*
Deutschland über alles.[43]
There in the ruins of his country
his city his childhood he forced
his memory on me making
his baggage my baggage making
me drop it and run. And I ran
for my life, but you cannot
run away from the child inside you:
I owe him I owe myself I owe
the children of my children
memory's lie detector test
bearing witness to what I know

to be true so that they can move on
on the conveyor belt of life
knowingly ignorant of the future
but forever sensible of who they are.

I returned next morning on a train
to Cologne more dead than alive
the relentless rhythm of the tracks
pounding pounding pounding
a message struggling to be heard
over blood-curdling sirens, the roar
of bomber formations, the screams,
the prayers that availed nothing
in the aching head pounding
to be understood between images
of dying, despair, destruction
the railroad pounding pounding
the mind's womb to generate
a genesis beyond guilt, terror
and persecution, beyond mirages
of memory and meaning, beyond
Nolde's twilight seas, Constable's
landscapes and Goya's *Pinturas
negras* to be reborn in a world
that can be trusted with the seasons
and with the torments of the heart.

Here where the last ice age melted
into the largest fresh water lakes
on the planet I saw the light again.
Like Alice I walked through a mirror
into my second coming, fittingly,

on All Fools' Day the year that certified
my maturity precisely as I set out
to find it on an Odyssey from the killing
cities of a continent out of joint
in search of a passage home
to the community of forests, rivers
and skies, to engage their discourse
with time and the wind and silence.

Now, half a century later, a hush
has settled on the past. In my dreams
explosions are flocks of lotus flowers
floating on an unfathomable sea.
They dip beneath the water's surface
in the evening when the sun paints
the clouds the blood of too many wars
to rise bright as water lilies when light
is born again to leap from wave to wave
up shores, bluffs and cliffs to lift
a continent out of darkness to glory.

Here too the grasping animal lost
its way and fared not much better.
Rattle snakes and black flies trouble
lovers, poison ivy has its season,
and winter wipes life's slate clean.
But here there are healing stones
too, and inside them healing silences
to which the wheel of good fortune
can raise the mind to gather strength
for the never ending journey
searching for a way that leads

beyond human understanding
that has brought us where we are.

It took four score years to learn
that to heal, to be whole I must
come to terms with the child
I once was and be reconciled
to the childhood that launched me
on the mind's quest for comprehension.
I am that child still, still learning to read
the signals at the intersection of many
eternities that marks the moving point
we call today, still learning to build
like the beaver a lodge that is home
in the wilderness of particles and poplars,
black holes and blizzards, quarks and quirks,
hypotheses and perceptions, still learning
to love all that is here and now or nothing.

In the old country I acquired a language
contaminated by years of deception;
in the new world I learnt to listen
to the trees whispering to the stars
in a soft breeze on a summer night,
to the surf blurting out what the fish
mouth to the ocean currents, to the rain
carrying mountains into valleys and
fetching blossoms from the darkness
to the light. Perhaps that's the secret:
to listen till your ears can pick up beyond
the foreground noise the hustle and bustle
in the assembly of numberless microbes

making and unmaking worlds without
beginning or end. They teach a language
for all seasons where words point beyond
what they name to where those who can
say yes to the world can step into the same
river time and again carrying the stars
to uncertain destinations, and then go back
to the drawing-board and design a future.

As the red river of the heart carried me
from the Rhine to the Ottawa I learnt
that rivers speak the same language
always and everywhere: they link the clouds
to the roots of all life on their way to the sea.

Endnotes

German phrases translated by the author

1   Poets and Thinkers
2   *Treasure Island* by R.L. Stevenson
3   *Winnitou,* a Wild West novel by Karl May that every German youngster read
4   King's Forest, an actual forest to the East of Cologne
5   Grandma
6   *Tsar and Carpenter,* an opera by Gustav Albert Lortzing
7   *Oh, I am clever and wise, and no one can deceive me,* an aria from Lortzing's opera
8   *The words were composed by me in a quiet hour,* another aria from Lortzing's opera
9   Daddy and Mummy
10   *Rustle of Spring,* Op. 32, No. 3, by Christian Sinding
11   cf. footnote 6

12	Slate pencil
13	(*literally*) little pee-man, a genial euphemism for a child's penis
14	You don't have any foreskin!
15	(*literally*) little flag leader = a rank in the Hitler Youth, equivalent to Squadron Leader
16	You're a loutish Jew!
17	(*literally*) Confinement to a room, equivalent to house arrest
18	(*literally*) ancestors' passport = a document, resembling a passport, required of every citizen in Nazi Germany, tracing a person's ancestry as far back as possible, supported by legal documents
19	Pound-cake with whipping cream
20	The reference is to Grimm's fairytale about *Die Bremer Stadtmusikanten* (The Town Musicians of Bremen)
21	This was possible due to a nation-wide, government-sponsored program (*Kinderlandverschickung*) which sent urban kids to farms in the country during the school holidays in the summer.

37	(*literally*) stumbling-stones: they were first introduced by Günter Demnig in Cologne in 1994 to create a memorial to the victims of the Nazi killing machine; they have since spread to many German cities *lest we forget*
38	Here lived / Aron Freund / born 1929 / deported 1941 / murdered
39	Subhumans
40	Supermen
41	...all humans become brothers... from Beethoven's *Ode to Joy* in his Symphony No. 9
42	...this kiss to the whole world... (*ibid*)
43	Germany, Germany above all – national anthem during the Nazi period. The tune came from Haydn's String Quartet, Op. 76, No. 3, and was originally adopted as the national anthem of Austria with the text: *Gott erhalte unseren Kaiser...* (God save our Emperor...)

Poetry Books by Henry Beissel:

Witness the Heart (1963)
New Wings for Icarus (1966)
The World is a Rainbow (1968)
The Price of Morning (translations, 1968)
Face on the Dark (1970)
The Salt I Taste (1975)
A Different Sun (translations, 1976)
Cantos North (1980, 1982)
Season of Blood (1984)
Poems New and Selected (1987)
Ammonite (1987)
A Thistle in his Mouth (translations, 1987)
Stones to Harvest (1987, 1993)
Dying I was Born (1992)
Letters on Birchbark (translations, 2000)
The Dragon & the Pearl (2002)
Across the Sun's Warp (2003)
The Meteorology of Love (2010)